LET'S GET

UN
STUCK

INTRODUCTION

The snow was coming down so thick, I could barely make out the silhouette of something - or someone. At first, I thought it might have been a wild animal, maybe a polar bear; but as he came into focus, I realized it was indeed the shape of a human, bent over sharply, covered in a blanket of snow, thigh deep in this frozen grave.

As he drew nearer, I realized that he had an enormous, gaping wound just to the left of his shoulder - or where his shoulder should have been. His shoulder and arm were missing and there was nothing but ice and exposed bone and cold, coagulated flesh. Except for his frosted face and his shoulder, the thick layers of skins seemed to give him ample shelter from the elements.

He slowly picked up his chin and I could finally make out his facial features. Behind his long black hair, matted with snow, was the face of a native American. The distinct weathered skin of a man who had endured pain and whose life was nearing the end unless he was rescued.

His dark eyes were dim but a glint of hope shone through. He could neither smile nor frown. He was emotionless: whether by frostbite or by exhaustion, I could not tell. Not a single muscle on his face gave any indication that he had seen me.

Around his neck and remaining shoulder hung a thick, knotted rope that swung behind him, leading to a wooden sled laying atop the soft snow. On this sled, what looked to be two dead bodies, wrapped tightly in a burlap-type material. Each wrapped individually, but tied to one another and then cinched down securely to the sled itself. Nothing else on the sled, except two frozen corpses.

When I awoke, it only took a few seconds to reorient myself to my surroundings... our bed, our room, our home. I was in a comfortable, warm, familiar place. The deep snow had drifted away, but the man in my dream would haunt me. I got up to get a drink and his deeply weathered face stared at me in the mirror.

I knew what the dream meant yet I was still full of questions. Would I tell Joy? Would I do anything about it? Would things ever get better?

I was that man, plodding through a cold existence with a death sentence. I was digging my own grave with every step. It was me. I had been mortally wounded by childhood rejection and teenage failure yet pressing on in exhaustion. I was a man dispossessed of my true inheritance by addiction. Yes, even the sled revealed my inability to truly deal with the grief of both my parent's untimely passing. I was dragging them around, unable to let go.

I was stuck. My mind was stuck. My emotions were stuck. It was affecting my health, my relationships. My marriage was suffering, my children were suffering, my job was suffering. I didn't realize it, but I was closer to self-destruction than I even realized at the time.

I had begun to hate myself, to grow weary of life, to resent my family, and worst of all to grow distant from God. Of course, this wasn't the first time, but this was the worst time. I was stuck.

Perhaps this book finds you stuck... stuck in shame or brokenness, stuck by abuse and abandonment, wounded by loss or loneliness, dragging around the weight of grief or addiction. Perhaps you connect with the tired Native American who was only a few more breaths alive than the two bodies he was dragging. Has the world become a cold grave to die in? Have you given into your frozen fate and resigned to the death inside?

If you feel like something in you has died, like you're walking wounded, or like you're dragging an unbearable weight around, this book is for you.

LET'S GET UNSTUCK... TOGETHER!

This is a kind of workbook ... or maybe more like a journal of sorts. We're not just going to get unstuck by reading something, we're going to have to put in a little more effort than that. At the conclusion of each chapter, I'm going to ask something of you. Sometimes it's simple and quick, a few of the challenges will be that - challenging. But I can honestly say, if you'll take the time, you WILL get unstuck. So, **ARE YOU READY?**

Your first unstuck assignment is to grab a pen and write in the word YES or NO to the question above. Then, clip your pin in the book so you'll have it for the end of our next chapter; you're gonna' need it!

Not long ago, I was reading a great book about counseling someone with PTSD. When I say great, that might be a stretch... it was more like a long, detailed, boring college textbook holding the promise of buried treasure scattered within this "comprehensive manual." I dug deep but what I discovered was gold. Here are the *cliff notes* version... you're welcome.

CHAPTER 1

STUCK POINTS

When an traumatic event occurs, how we respond in the days and weeks following will impact the rest of our lives. How we process through what happened to us, or even what we did to someone else, has to power to shape vastly different outcomes. It can either bring life or death. A teen girl is raped. A soldier experiences his first fire-fight. A drunk driver T-bones a family. An officer is fired upon. A mother screams insults at her children. A CFO makes the wrong call and upends everything. An orphan quits calling for his mommy. A man wheels his SUV into the strip club for the first time. A nurse loses her first patient. A new widow cries herself to sleep. A student takes his first hit. A daughter stops praying for her daddy to come home. A pastor throws in the towel. A man finds his escape in the barrel of a gun.

If you've lived very long, I am certain that you have experienced a wounding event. Probably enough that you could be diagnosed with PTSD or at least some form of acute stress disorder (i.e. - anxiety, depression). What you might not realize is how powerful your response is to such trauma.

How did you handle what happened to you? What did you think about what happened? How did it change your beliefs about yourself, about God, about the world?

Think about what you're going through like ABC: Action (the defining event), Belief (what you think about the event), and Consequence (what you are feeling or doing now). The action was the traumatic thing you experienced. The belief is how you processed what happened in the first few days and weeks. The consequence is how you're coping with it today.

[A] ACTION - the traumatic, wounding event

[B] BELIEF - what you think about what happened [A]

[C] CONSEQUENCE - how you feel about [A] and what you end up doing as a result of [B]

If you've ever been to counseling, perhaps you have dug into some of this before. But most of the time we try to deal with it ourselves. We tend to focus on the event [A] and how we feel about it or the habits that have come from it [C], not realizing that the [B] is really the most important! We tend to wish A (the event) never happened and dream of a life without [A] (the trauma) but that gets us nowhere. In reality, our [C] (emotional way of coping) is to avoid the thought or the create new feelings about the victim or the oppressor. We might even create new habit or routines to avoid the trigger or arousal of the sheer pain of our traumatic wound (for example: strong negative emotions, social withdrawal, substance abuse, bingeing, avoidance, self-harm, aggression).

But we need to take a closer look at our new beliefs [B] that are formed by such an event [A]. We should take another look at what we believe about the traumatic and turbulent time and **revisit how we responded and/or reacted internally to such negative stimulation.** Traumatic experiences have a way of rewiring the brain and creating new neural pathways that almost immediately create new patterns of thinking, new beliefs, new absolutes in our psyche that could be as damaging (or more so) than the traumatic event itself. This is called a stuck point.

Stuck points are not the new behaviors and feelings [C] that have come from our trauma, they are the core beliefs [B] that changed due to the pain. Stuck points are new thoughts that took shape and solidified as a result of the fire of that particular trial. For example, a stuck point is not the addiction but the cause of addiction. Stuck points are at the root from which grows the fruit. Stuck points are not actions or feelings (both of which are byproducts of thoughts).

Stuck points are thoughts about yourself, about life, or about God.

LET'S GET UNSTUCK

In order to really go further, you're going to have to take a few minutes (more than a few, actually) and write a few paragraphs (a page, ideally) about your traumatic event. **You're not being asked to write specifics but focus on WHY the event occurred. Write about what caused the event.** If you might have more than one, then you're going to need to pick one event. Choose either the first one or the one that you thought of first as one of the most significant. We can work through others later. Please go ahead a write it. It's important... I'll wait.

Note: "Stuck point" and the "ABC" model were originally coined by Patricia A. Resick, in her book "Cognitive Processing Therapy for PTSD"

"You shall know the Truth and the Truth shall set you free! So if the Son sets you free, you will be free indeed." -Jesus

CHAPTER 2

THE POWER OF TRUTH

We live in a day where truth is bendable. I can't understand how truths like "Concrete is hard" or "Fire is hot" can be flexible... but - in this day and to this generation - they are. We even use phrases like *'your truth'* and *'my truth'* to describe two versions of the same story.

If we're going to get unstuck, we've got to grasp a new concept... actually a very old concept. **Truth is absolute.** Truth does not bend, not even for me or you. Truth is solid and unchanging. Truth is truth and that's the truth! Watch this... if you say that the truth is there is no such thing as absolute truth, then just ask yourself: "Are you absolutely sure? Is that the truth?" It doesn't work that way!

Truths are unchanging. They can't be bought or bent, they may go out of style but they're never out-dated. We get stuck when our opinions become our 'truths' instead of the truths formulating our opinions. When our beliefs [B] about ourselves, life, and God try to reshape the truth, then we stop growing and get stuck.

For example, one of the greatest truths is: 'You were made by God, in His image. He loves you because He's good like that.' But our experiences whisper (and sometimes scream) shame and condemnation. We begin to feel unlovable, especially by Someone who claims to know every part of us, inside and out. Our new *truth* becomes that we WERE loved, but not any more. But the reality is that's not real truth, that's just our feeling that we've substituted for the facts.

The problem is that wounds of pain and trauma will cause us to replace those solid truths with our own new beliefs and we don't even realize we've done it. We've switched life-long, rock-hard facts for the shifting sand of feelings as our foundation.

In his most famous sermon, Jesus said that everyone will experience life's storms and floods. We will all experience the wind and rain. What matters is our foundation. What really matters is the truth.

All I'm suggesting is that agree with the truth and not try to rewrite it. What has God already said about you, about Himself, and about this life?

When you think about what has happened to you... the pain, the trauma, the event(s) [A] that changed your life's course, what "I" statements did you tell yourself about it? I've included a few stuck points that are likely your opinions [B] that you've replaced to become your new foundation for surviving [C].

Mark the one(s) that hit closest to home with you:

___ If only I had done better or been more vigilant...
___ I messed up and _____ happened
___ Because I didn't tell anyone...
___ I should have known what would happen
___ It's my fault
___ If I had been paying attention
___ I don't deserve to be happy
___ If I let other people get close to me...
___ If I hadn't been drinking / taken that _____
___ No one can understand me
___ I am unlovable
___ I am worthless
___ I am damaged goods
___ I deserve all the bad things that happen to me
___ I must control what happens to me from here on out
___ I can't trust anyone
___ I have no control over my future
___ I'm a terrible person
___ I am a pervert
___ I'm a lost cause

CONFESSION

When you and I think of confession, we're likely thinking of someone uncovering a huge secret or bringing to light a hidden darkness. That's not really it at all. What people don't understand about confession is that it literally means *"to agree"* / *"to say the same thing as."* It's more about my mind coming into agreement with the truth that never changes. It's about me moving toward the Light. Confession is when I come to a place to recognize that 'my truth' is nothing more than an improper opinion and that I need to let it go and replace it with a real truth.

It's time for you to get unstuck. It's time for you to identify one or more of those beliefs [B] that have drug you down for too long. It's time for you to agree with God about who you are. Which one(s) will you topple over today?

It's time to challenge those beliefs with some truth! Ask yourself... 'Is that opinion really the fact or is that a feeling based on what happened to me? Do most people who know me and who care about me feel that way too? Is it helpful for me to rehearse that statement or is it harmful? What can I tell myself on such occasions in the future?' And here's the big one: ***'What is the truth that I should replace this statement with?'***

Google it. I do it all the time, along with millions of other people. And if you can't find a simple, truth-filled statement, then I've included a few on the last page of this chapter. I like to call them myth-busters. They are the promises of God found in His Word.

LET'S GET UNSTUCK

To get unstuck, you must replace a belief with truth. You must. You can't get unstuck by letting that lie hold you back any longer. So do it, right now. Please take a second and whisper the old belief. Then say the new truth that will replace it a little louder. Repeat it even louder again. For real, say it with your lips (not just with the voice in your head).

Take the next step: write it down. In the space below, write down what you said with your mouth a moment ago. Better yet, don't just write it and keep it a secret; also send it in a text, on a postcard, or maybe even on social media. Confess the Truth as your truth. Be specific and don't be ashamed. Agree with God about it. It's true already, so claim it as yours... because it is!

MYTH-BUSTERS

God is with you: "I will never leave you or forsake you"

You were made in God's image: "So God created mankind in his own image, in the image of God he created them; male and female he created them."

Things happen for a reason: "All things work together for good"

You are loved: "For I am convinced that neither death nor life, neither angels nor demons, neither the present nor the future, nor any powers, neither height nor depth, nor anything else in all creation, will be able to separate us from the love of God that is in Christ Jesus our Lord."

You were made for a purpose: "We are his handiwork, created unto good works"

You are loved: "This is how God showed his love among us: He sent his one and only Son into the world that we might live through him."

God is greater than anything in this world: "Greater is He that is in you than he that is in the world"

God's thoughts are on you: "I know the thoughts I think toward you…to give you a future and a hope"

You are loved: "And so we know and rely on the love God has for us. God is love."

CHAPTER 3

THE POWER OF LOVE

You are loved. You are known and still, you are loved. I can't say it enough because we can't hear it enough. In this world where everything is transactional and conditional, there is one thing that is so unearthly and beautiful: God's love.

LOVE IS LIGHT.
FEAR IS DARKNESS.
RUN TO THE LIGHT.

Several times in the Old Testament, a peculiar request is made: "God, make your face to shine on us." It is usually connected with the ideas of God's love and grace. When God's shining face is mentioned in the Psalms and Torah, the one writing is usually in a time of trouble or crisis. They are needing something — something big… and so they ask for *[drumroll please]* God's shining face! Why? Because His face shining IS big, really big!

GOD'S SMILE IS NOT A RESPONSE TO OUR GOOD ACTIONS. IT IS A CAUSATIVE FORCE FOR OUR GOOD & FOR HIS GLORY.

When I smile at my children, it's usually a reflection of their behavior. Usually. But sometimes, I just smile at them because they are mine and they make me happy. I've caught myself smiling at them when they're sleeping. God's smile is born in His heart of grace toward His creation and children – not in our behavior. He can smile on us and be gracious to us even when we're not deserving of it. That's what grace is… when we were sinners, Christ dying for us. When we would never had chosen Him, He reached toward us. I think that's why the Bible says God 'makes' His face to shine on us; we don't deserve it, but God really wants to give it to us, so He wills it.

GOD'S SHINING FACE HAS THE POWER TO CHANGE THINGS, TO MOVE PEOPLE, TO IMPACT ME AND MY WORLD.

I challenge you to receive and accept God's love for you right now. If you have never let His smile make you smile, then -by faith- take that step. Below is a sample prayer of faith. It's a simple statement of dependence on God to do what we cannot do:

Dear Jesus, I believe that You are God, that You died for my failures and sins, and that You are alive again. I don't know all the details but I'm trusting in You. I can't do it on my own, I need a Rescue. I need You. Please come into my life. Amen.

Your beliefs [B] will determine your behavior [C]. Our beliefs are the grid on which our behavior is built. Your attitudes will affect your actions – often unconsciously. We don't even really have to try – we act out what we think. If a person believes that mutual fund investing is a great idea, he will find the money to invest. If parents feel that God's word is important, they will find ways to integrate it into the lives of their children. If you believe Jesus is the only way to Heaven, you will do what He says to get there… makes sense!

"INTEGRITY IS KEEPING THE PROMISES YOU MAKE TO YOURSELF." -DICK SAVAGE

The problem enters when we don't behave like we believe. We say that we believe something – yet we behave differently. For example, a husband might say that he values his wife, yet if he doesn't make her a priority, he will not find the happiness in his identity as a husband. Emotions go all wrong when our grid [B] doesn't match our life [C] – when what we value and what we do don't line up. This happens all the time in marriages, in politics, and in our relationship with God – doesn't it?! That's why John said:

...LET US NOT LOVE IN WORD, NEITHER IN TONGUE; BUT IN DEED AND IN TRUTH. 1 JOHN 3:18B

Life is built so that your inner-most values might guide and govern your lifestyle. When these two are in line, there is great joy and your feelings are satisfied. When what you believe and what you do aren't together, you begin to feel like you're investing in things that do not matter. This only brings more frustration, anger, and bitterness against those you love (or even against yourself).

LET'S GET UNSTUCK

Now it's time for a quick exercise: Write down the two or three things that are most important to you – right now. If it's a relationship, then determine what you can do for that person today. Take a step – just one. What promise of quitting did you make to yourself? or of starting a new habit? It's go-time! If it's a spiritual calling, then find a Scripture that will fuel your vision to go forward. Write it down and put the date by it. You'll get so much joy and satisfaction from investing effort into what's important to you.

_____

_____

_____

_____

PART 2

You're halfway there! In the first half of this book, we have focused on the ABC's (Action, Belief, and Consequence) of true therapeutic healing. Now is the time for me to stop you and to ask if you're ready to move forward?

Two HUGE secrets to getting unstuck are **direction and momentum**. Let me explain: When you're stuck, you're focused on your location. You see where you want to be and you get discouraged or disillusioned. Without even realizing it, you could fail to see the importance of the slight changes in your direction, missing how important just one degree of change will accomplish. So far, you've made three tiny course corrections and you've got some momentum. You're getting unstuck and you might not even realize it yet!

The next few chapters are all about keeping up that momentum and tweaking your direction even further.

BEFORE MOVING FORWARD, A WARNING

Is there something holding still you back? A warning: the next two or three chapters are especially hard to hear if you've not identified a few of your stuck points, but the advice will change your life if you will act on them. I'm not going to try to talk you out of reading further, I just know that a review of part one might be better for some readers than what's next...

A man had two sons. The younger son told his father, 'I want my share of your estate now before you die.' So his father agreed to divide his wealth between his sons. "A few days later this younger son packed all his belongings and moved to a distant land, and there he wasted all his money in wild living. About the time his money ran out, a great famine swept over the land, and he began to starve. He persuaded a local farmer to hire him, and the man sent him into his fields to feed the pigs. The young man became so hungry that even the pods he was feeding the pigs looked good to him. But no one gave him anything. He finally came to his senses...

So he returned home to his father. And while he was still a long way off, his father saw him coming. Filled with love and compassion, he ran to his son, embraced him, and kissed him. His son said to him, 'Father, I have sinned against both heaven and you, and I am no longer worthy of being called your son.' "But his father said to the servants, 'Quick! Bring the finest robe in the house and put it on him. Get a ring for his finger and sandals for his feet. And kill the calf we have been fattening. We must celebrate with a feast, for this son of mine was dead and has now returned to life. He was lost, but now he is found.' So the party began.

-Jesus, Luke 15

CHAPTER 4

THE POWER OF GRACE

Luke 15 is known as the story of the Prodigal Son. Many think the word 'prodigal' has to do with the sin of being far from home, but the meaning goes much deeper than that! Prodigal literally means *extravagant; wasteful; reckless.*

Prodigal most often is applied to the attitude of the Son toward his inheritance that should've landed him on the Jerry Springer show, yet I'd love to change your mind on that. Have you ever considered that there was another in this story more extravagant, more reckless with the inheritance? Consider the FATHER! Which of you dads would grant the same request to your 21 year old son? Which of you would give half of what you own – a hard-earned living – just to be squandered away? I wouldn't have, I know that. I'm appalled when I hear Dave Ramsey say that the average time for kids to spend their inheritance (60 years of saving) is only 18 months!

But that is the point of the story… this is about God and His parenting grace. **GRACE:** God's goodness that is free of charge, no strings attached, on the house; the riches of God that scream to be abused; the undeserved favor of God that cannot be defined or captured by words; the unconditional love of God that is so often spurned; the acceptance of God that may or may not be accepted.

In a world of un-grace, where you hear: "no free lunch, you get what you deserve, earn your respect" … we can tend to parent the same. But God doesn't parent that way – He is radically different… He parents with far less control that I exert, and with much more free will than I extend, and is perfectly consistent with the consequences. He considers the actions of his children, but they never dictate his response. He operates full of both grace and truth. Have you ever had a person extend that much grace to you? If so, how did you react? How will you respond to such grace from God right now?

ACCEPTANCE

People like Oprah and Dr. Phil are mainstreaming the idea that we cannot truly forgive anyone else unless we first forgive ourselves. We have all tried to apologize to someone only to have them refuse it. I have longed to say that I'm sorry after it's too late and they're gone. I know what it's like to need to hear that I'm forgiven and to never have the satisfaction. And that's why I can't stop punishing myself for my mistakes.

The reason that it's so hard to forgive yourself is because it's impossible! You and I can't set ourselves free—no more than a prisoner can will himself outside of the bars and razor-wire. Freedom must come from a higher authority—from God. The Bible never mentions forgiving yourself. Not one time. Our need is forgiveness, but not the kind you can give yourself… but the freedom that God gives.

Jesus also told the story of a servant who owed the king $15 million—but was totally forgiven. He could not repay, yet due to the kindness of the King, he would not have to! This servant then went out found a fellow-servant, grabbed him by the throat, and demanded $5,000 from him. Since the debtor could not repay, he was cast into prison. When the King heard the news, He demanded that his servant be brought to Him. Since this man received grace and forgiveness, yet could not grant the same, he would be judged.

You and I have been totally forgiven. Our sins have been paid for. That's why Jesus Christ died on the cross—to suffer the punishment that you and I deserve. Just like He accepted the blame so that we would not have to, we must accept what He did as the payment for our sins. I met a man a few months ago that told me he was good enough to get to heaven. It shocked me! He said that he was a good man—better than most — and that he thought that was enough. I asked him, "If we can be good enough to get to Heaven, then why did Jesus have to die?" He replied, "That's easy, for the bad ones." What he was saying was that he did not need (nor accept) what Jesus did for him. He did not want God's charity. Until we experience God's forgiveness, we will never be able to forgive those who hurt us.

To forgive someone is to set them free. We set them free of the penalty and debt that they owe us. When you have been wronged, something has been taken from you, someone has damaged you, injured you, or taken advantage of you—the greatest thing you will ever do is to let go. To forgive. To set them free. It's easier said than done, isn't it? Even though we know it's the right thing to do, that doesn't mean we will—sometimes I want to forgive and feel like I can't! It's not just a switch that I can flip and just, poof, there it is. It's not that easy, and God knows that! He understands, that's why He always links your decision to forgive another to a motivator (blessing) or a consequence (curse).

FOR IF YOU FORGIVE OTHERS THEIR OFFENSES, YOUR HEAVENLY FATHER WILL FORGIVE YOU AS WELL. BUT IF YOU DON'T FORGIVE OTHERS, YOUR FATHER WILL NOT FORGIVE YOUR OFFENSES. -JESUS

The funny thing about forgiveness is that it doesn't just set them free, it sets you free, too. It frees you from the acid of resentment. It allows the wound to begin healing. When you forgive, you release yourself from negative emotions that will hold you hostage. The Bible is very clear about how bitterness will continue to cut and hurt your spirit (Hebrews 12:15). But that's not all... the Scriptures teach that if the grudge isn't dealt with, it's toxins will leak out of our lives and ruin those closest to us.

Who is it that you're letting hold you back? What grudge is it that's keeping you stuck? Is there a tiny measure of bitterness you're not letting go of because to do so would violate your strong sense of justice (or maybe even vengeance) for that person?

LET'S GET UNSTUCK

Take a minute and process back through those questions again, jotting down any event or person that comes to your mind. Next, doodle a cage (like a birdcage or a prison door) NEXT to the name of the offender or the wounding event. It's a symbol that you are setting them free from your resentment ...and thereby setting yourself free, too! It will be a reminder to your future self that you've already set them free, you can't be locking them up again just because you're having a bad day. See why it's so important? So if you didn't do it yet, what are you waiting for?

Resist the Devil and He will flee from you.
 - James 4:7

CHAPTER 5

THE POWER OF PROCRASTINATION

"Not right now."

These three words are a powerful tool for any parent. If you have kids, then you know exactly what I'm talking about! It's easier than saying *'No'* to their request, but it almost certainly means *No*. Why? Because my kids tend to be fickle and out-of-sight-out-of-mind. Kind of like me. If I can delay, the request loses its power, and they move on.

NOT RIGHT NOW

I've recently discovered that these three words work in my struggle with temptation, with cravings, and with unhealthy appetites of any kind. It really is the easiest way to say, *No*. For me, saying *No* is difficult.

I've waged a war against the devil in my head and resisted about all that I can while I'm being told that I'll never be able to stand. At the same time, I'm telling myself to be strong, but I also hear the voice that asks how long I can last. I hear the whisper that it's a losing battle.

LET'S GET UNSTUCK

So the next time you're tempted, instead of saying *No* and arguing until you're worn down into surrender, just say *"Not right now!"* Just put the craving off until later. Out of sight, out of mind. When I do, I'm not assuming that I will cave later on, I'm assuming that I'll have more grace and greater strength then to say it again and again. I'm hopeful that my 'passive-aggressive resistance' be enough that he'll move on – and it usually works! The truth is, I don't have enough sovereignty to be sure that my *No* really means *No* any other time than now… **All I can do is say *No* for now.**

Don't let the Devil use tomorrow against you anymore (Matthew 6:34). So just put it off now – and then keep putting it off again and again… forever! Delay the gratification and just keep delaying it. Many times, it's easier than trying to draw a definitive line in the sand in the face of your worst enemy with a grip on your Achilles' heel. Maybe later you'll be stronger, maybe later you will have help, maybe later… *just not right now!*

CHAPTER 6

THE POWER OF LITTLE THINGS

Recently, I have taken up the challenge attempting to change my body. I was quite tired of the way I looked and frustrated that it kept getting worse. I found myself well over 300 pounds and the more I thought about it the more I ate. I remembered the words of the old preacher who would look down at his gut, patting it with loving affection, and say, *"It's hard to believe I built that with a spoon!"*

I had to tell myself over and over that I didn't get here overnight, and I wouldn't get back that fast either. I got myself stuck one day, one bad decision at a time. If I was going to get unstuck, it would have to be the same way... one decision, one day at a time.

GOOD THINGS TAKE TIME.

And now, six months later, I can say that things have turned around a little bit more. I'm down 35 pounds and changing my body shape. I'm enjoying going to the gym and learning to make better choices for myself. I don't have a diet secret to share with you, nobody's going to be beating down my door finding out how, and I haven't yet amassed a social media following of willing disciples. It's been through hard work five times a week at the gym and in caloric moderation (only one donut instead of six!). I'm sure I could've been further ahead if I had done keto, but I know me and I know that it wouldn't last.

DON'T BE AFRAID OF GOING SLOWLY; BE AFRAID OF STANDING STILL.

The only way out is one step at a time. Your traumatic, wounding event might have impacted your direction, but it did not dictate your steps. Stop blaming that thing, that person. Now is time to take responsibility for today and take a step in the right direction.

In life, you get to choose your 'hard.' It's not always easy to wake up and go to the gym, but it's not easy to wake up overweight and hating to look in the mirror. My muscles are sore if I work out, my joints are sore if I don't... I get to choose my hard. It's the same with money... trying to be responsible adults with our money is no fun, but neither is being up to the gills in debt! I get to choose my hard. Marriage isn't easy but divorce isn't the greener grass many hope for.

You get to choose your hard. Confronting painful issues from your past isn't any harder than trying to ignore them. **Choose your hard.**

What can one step do?

It might not be your weight. Maybe it's infidelity. Maybe it's alcohol. Or maybe it's a destructive thought pattern that's got you stuck in your head. It could be worry and fear... or perhaps anger. Whatever it is, you're not going to move forward unless you take a step. Take one step. Just one. Take it...

LET'S GET UNSTUCK

My wife reminds me more often than I'd like to admit that the little things matter the most. I'm a big picture guy who often overlooks the details, but the little things matter. Little things add up. Little things make a big difference. Little things show big heart.

List 2-3 small steps that you could take today (below). Now scratch through all but one. This is the one, the one step you're going to take today to get unstuck.

_____

_____

_____

_____

Lord, make me aware of my end and the number of my days so that I will know how short-lived I am. In fact, you have made my days just inches long, and my life span is as nothing to you. Yes, every human being stands as only a vapor. *Selah*

Now, Lord, what do I wait for? My hope is in you. Rescue me from all my transgressions; do not make me the taunt of fools.
Hear my prayer, LORD, and listen to my cry for help; do not be silent at my tears.

-David, Psalm 39

CHAPTER 7

THE POWER OF HOPE

Not long ago, I was having a really hard day that was made public and many people reached out to me, asking *"How are you?"* They offered prayers and encouragement, but I didn't really know how to answer... then the Lord spoke. He blended the memory of my son's birthday with the inspired Word from the thirty-ninth Psalm. David was low and felt the pain of difficult relationships, yet he prayed that God would help him guard his words. He was tempted to be overwhelmed by this earthly struggle, but God revealed to him how short that life really is. He concluded that this life is only a vapor, a shadow... mere inches on a timeline of eternity! Yet what did he need to do? Wait. Just stop and wait and pray and trust.

This life is so short... too short to waste. So how do

we make the most of it?

By waiting. Yes, waiting on God, hoping in God, trusting in God.

I know that sounds counter-intuitive. Normally, most people would follow *'Life is short'* with *'go, hurry, run!'* But God presents a different reality: **this life is NOT all there is.** There's more going on that what you see. There's more happening that what you feel. There's more at stake than what you first thought. The inches of this life will eternally impact the rest of your existence. So stop. Wait on God. Hope in God. Trust Him. Quit trusting in your judgment alone. Stop feeling secure in your job and bank balance. Stop hoping in the temporary things of this earth.

THIS LIFE IS NOT ALL THERE IS.
THERE'S MORE GOING ON THAT WHAT YOU SEE.

A day later, on my son, Aaron's, eighth birthday. Just before bedtime, we sat him down at the kitchen table, singing to him, about to present him with a gift. He sat, surrounded by his loving family, full of joy and life… waiting with a grin. He didn't know what was next but he knew it would be good. He trusted that he has good parents who wanted to give him good gifts. He wasn't nervous or tense. He waited patiently, smiling the entire time.

LET'S GET UNSTUCK

In this phase of life, you've been set down at the table. Look around and you'll see people who love you, full of joy and life… and you're waiting with a grin. I don't know what's next but I know it's going to be good! Will you trust that you have a good Father who wants to give you good gifts. So there's no need to be nervous or tense (mostly!). Let's go forward, dwelling in hope… won't you join me?!

What's something you're waiting on? Are you waiting with a grin?

_____

_____

_____

_____

_____

For God has not given us a spirit of fear, but one of power, love, and sound judgment. – The Apostle, 2 Timothy 1:7

If we don't learn from our experiences, we are sure to experience them again and again. And if they're failures, that's not good news!

CHAPTER 8

THE POWER OF FAILURE

Success and failure aren't mutually exclusive.
It's not either-or.

I was raised thinking that I was either a success OR a failure, but that's a lie. They can exist in the same person, side-by-side. In the same relationships, in the same marriage, at work, in your ministry, in your spirit, and in life. It's likely a team experiences both success and failure in season – even in a single game.

This isn't just a possibility, it is a reality. But it isn't just *a* reality, it is *the* reality. And what's awesome news is that it's not just reality... it's actually healthy! **How I recognize and handle my failures as they come is an often-overlooked key to more success!**

TODAY, I HOPE FOR YOUR SAKE THAT YOU EXPERIENCE BOTH SUCCESS & FAILURE!

I tend to be a person who gets down on myself quickly, someone who can get defensive and insecure about my abilities. These are the lies that failure tells: *You can't, you never will, you won't, you should not have even tried... It's hopeless.* If you hear that voice, it's not the voice of truth. It's not God's voice. It's not reality. Fight fire with fire. Fight the toxic doubt with life-giving truth of God's voice. This is another reason why the Bible is so important to me. It secures me in my true identity. It gives me a grid to build my life upon. This idea is really plowing through me right now (in trying to create, to write, to fix up my house, and to lead).

FAILURE IS AN OPPORTUNITY TO LEARN.

As we grow in this pattern, then we begin to understand about success and failure. Success is pleasing God – not reaching 'your number' before retirement. Success is passing a heritage of godliness to your children, not just handing them a 6-figure inheritance. Having said that, failure needs redefined by the Book too. Failure is not making a mistake. A failure is an opportunity to learn. Ever thought about this... scientists don't fail, they experiment!

When it comes to failure, here are my goals (borrowed from Jon Acuff & others):
• If I'm going to fail, I'm going to 'fail forward' (If I fail doing something that matters, then it's not a failure. If I set my goals high, I will not always reach them, but I will achieve more than if I had-

n't set them at all.)
- If I'm going to fail, I'm not going to let that stop me (Failure is quitting, staying down, not getting back up.)
- I should fear this: Succeeding at what doesn't matter! (The worst kind of failure is when I get good at something that has no real significance. It is when I am exalted at a position that has no bearing on eternity.)

LET'S GET UNSTUCK

What failure in your life are you avoiding? Which defeat are you trying to distance yourself from? What loss are you just trying to forget? It's likely you'll repeat history if you don't learn at least one simple lesson from it. I'll readily admit that many times I don't see the lesson that's right in front of my face – so I need to hear someone else say it. Perhaps you need to ask a mentor, a pastor, a coach, a true friend.

Here's where the rubber meets the road. It's time to reach out to someone who you respect, someone who will shoot you straight, and just say (or text): "Hey, I'm struggling right now and feel like I've made of mess of _____. From your perspective, how can I improve?" Write down their answer:

_____

_____

_____

So God created man in his own image; he created him in the image of God; he created them male and female. God blessed them, and God said to them, "Be fruitful, multiply, fill the earth, and subdue it. -Genesis 1:27-28

But Moses asked God, "Who am I that I should go to Pharaoh...? God replied to Moses, "I AM WHO I AM. This is what you are to say to the Israelites: I AM has sent me to you." -Exodus 3:11, 14

Thou art worthy, O Lord, to receive glory and honor and power: for thou hast created all things, and for thy pleasure they are and were created. -Revelation 4:11

CHAPTER 9

THE POWER OF IDENTITY

There are three basic types of people in this world – motivated by different things… Which one are you?

___ **Thinkers**. Thinkers are educators, philosophers, authors, pastors, politicians. They believe knowledge is power and want to help others know what they know.

___ **Fighters**. Fighters operate with a deep sense of courage and responsibility. These everyday warriors care about defending the defenseless and protecting others. They are cops, soldiers, and fire fighters.

___ **Doers**. Doers must be part of the action and are very results-oriented. Farmers, laborers, and factory workers make the world go around.

Knowing *HOW* God made you is important in answering the question *WHY* He made you. The danger is that **culture wants to redefine you**. This world's fads would try to erase how you were made and rewrite a new identity.

'Counterfeit' identities are offered by your Enemy on the following bases:

<u>Pleasure</u> (Happiness) – I'm the life of the party – I'm all about being happy & making people happy.

<u>Possessions</u> (Wealth) – I'm afraid that people won't love me if I don't pick up the tab.

<u>Position</u> (Accomplishments) – The size of my office and my trophy shelf give me a sense of importance.

<u>Power</u> (Authority) – I feel valuable because of the things I can do for others.

<u>Performance</u> (Success, Failure) – I worry that my foreclosure will cost me friendships.

Which 'counterfeit identity' is the most tempting for you to accept? *(circle the one you most identify with)*

YOLO

I'm sure you've run into YOLO, even if you didn't know it at first. YOLO means *'You Only Live Once.'* It's the mantra of the modern generation. Live for the moment. Live for your happiness. Go for what you want and don't look back. Get all you can, can all you get, and sit on the can! YOLO.

But just because it's popular doesn't make it right. The Apostle Paul said, in Romans 1, that living for pleasure apart from God ends in destruction – every time. I will never find fulfillment, satisfaction, or happiness in things here. I will never find anything that will give me a solid sense of identity apart from God. **Any real identity begins with God. It begins with how God relates to me and what God has assigned to me.**

Through a burning bush, God called Moses to lead His people. Moses asked a simple question of identity: "Who Am I?" (see Exodus 3) The answer came back through the fire: "I Am." At first, it doesn't seem like God answers Moses' question – but He did. He gave us the pattern to searching out the answer to the question of our identity…

MY 'I AM' BEGINS IN HIS 'I AM'

The 'I Am' is the name of God that represents his eternal, all-powerful, self-sufficient faithfulness. He is Life – unchangeable, uninterrupted, and immutable. My identity begins there.

I must realize that I've been uniquely created in His image to glorify Him (Ps 139:15-18). I am not a cosmic accident. I didn't just arrive here by chance. I owe God something. I am an Image-bearer – that tells me who I am. God knew me before I was known! Before I was named or known on earth, before I every knew my favorite color or flavor, before I lost my first tooth, before I worked my first job, before I experienced my first kiss, He knew me and had already determined my identity.

LET'S GET UNSTUCK

I really can't go any further in getting unstuck until I come to terms with the purpose of my existence. He has set the course of my life that I should live for His pleasure, and not mine only. And you, too. He has planted certain loves, tailored passions, and specific drives in you... So are you fulfilling that calling? Are you living up to my purpose as an image-bearer?

Here's a simple exercise to get us thinking about identity... Write a 140-character-max biography of yourself. Here's mine: "believer, family man, question-asker, communicator, hope-seeker, lover of chai, dark chocolate fanatic" As you can see, I like simple and to-the-point; no fluff. It only took me 42 tries to get it the way I want it.

Write your 1st draft here:

_____

_____

Now write a revised, better, updated bio here:

_____

_____

CHAPTER 10

THE POWER OF
GIVING YOURSELF A BREAK

"I'm not perfect, just forgiven. Haven't yet arrived, but I'm on my way…"

The lyrics to that old Joe Hemphill song, featured on Gaither's 2002 "I'll Fly Away" recording, is what I woke up to this morning. The radio wasn't on, nor my iPhone. It was on repeat in my head. It's what the Bible calls *sanctification*: the process of becoming holy.

On my journey, I have disappointed so many people. I've thought I was doing right, but I was deceived. At other times, I knew that I was doing wrong, and I kept it up anyway. But thank God – by His grace – that He never gives up on us and continues His work to perfect (mature) us until the day we will meet Him (Philippians 1:6). He's so amazing at accomplishing His will / work in us that He can even weave in the negative, dark, and ugly parts of our lives into the fabric of our life's mosaic.

As I continue to search and grow, I'm sure that I'm making mistakes along the way. I continue to make mistakes, to fail, to sin, and to let people down. (In case you haven't figured out – 'letting people down' is my biggest fear.) But it's my prayer that if I continue, by faith, to understand and obey His word that He will, by grace, overcome my imperfections and make me into a holy son. I believe that. I have to… because there's nothing I can do to make myself any holier. I know – been there, done that, doesn't work.

Think about this… God desires you to be perfect and complete and holy even more than you do! For the believer, every day is a step in that direction because we are promised the Holy Spirit. One of the most repeated commands to Christians in the New Testament is the simple word: "Let…" It's just that simple. Let God have his way. Allow the Spirit to work things for your good. Yield to what He wants to do in and through you. Let Him.

So if you're struggling today with your desire to be a finished work and no longer a work in progress, just remember that God enjoys the process. He didn't create the earth in 1 day, He took His time. For Him, that meant six days. He first formed the earth, then filled it. He first formed the seas, then filled them. He formed the skies, then filled them. He formed man, then filled him. So God is enjoying forming and filling you! Sit back and trust Him. Do your best to trust Him and to live a godly life – but rest in the reality that He is bringing His desire to pass on you (Jer. 29:11).

LET'S GET UNSTUCK

In what way can you give yourself a break? What are you not 'letting' God do with you today? Write down your prayer of where you commit to simply 'Let go and let God.'

Dear God,

_____

_____

_____

_____

_____

_____

- Amen

Made in the USA
Columbia, SC
31 December 2020

30099434R00030